Excerpts from an Overthinker's Pen

Sukanya Bhattacharyya

BookLeaf
Publishing

India | USA | UK

Presentation by *BookLeaf Publishing*

Web: www.bookleafpub.com

E-mail: info@bookleafpub.com

ISBN: 978-93-5744-936-6

First edition 2022

DEDICATION

This book is dedicated to my family and especially my mother. They have always been my strength and inspiration. They will always be the driving force behind my dreams coming true and my goals turning into achievements.

ACKNOWLEDGEMENT

{{Acknowledgement}}Thank You to BookLeaf Publishing for helping me take a step towards creating and keeping up with a hobby so close to my heart.
Thank you to the readers, for going through these pages of nuances. Most of all, thank you to Sneha, Anushka and Natasha, my best friends, my family- life would just not be the same without you.

PREFACE

This book is a product of a perpetual thirst of creation and penning down of emotions. Every poem leads to self-reflection in one way or another. Written during the unexpected shutting down of the world towards the end of 2019 and the beginning of 2020, this book is a collection of some of the thoughts that each of us faced, consciously or subconsciously.

Tired

My home… My little piece…
I have been away,
To seek some chaos, some sunlight…
Far away, at the bay,
Now that I see you…
Will you let me stay?
Now that you see me by your window again…
Will you indeed let me stay?
I will run down the old steps with you…
Build back those broken pots of clay,
I will buy you new paints…
Will you use my hues for your foyer?
The fireflies we counted…
I'll fill the glass jars again if you say!!
Well at least let me keep looking from here at you,
With you I shall decay!
I'm but homeless without you,
Rent to your lost eyes I'll pay!!

Immortal

For the heavens know,
How you come and go...

In the quiet of a crowded street,
In the heat of a chilly night,
In the storm of a calm breeze,
In the dark of a day, shining bright!!

A bubble a day, time bursts along the way,
A twig a day, time grows upon my crown,
Have I given up too much today?
Am I going to visit another town?

The only letters that remain,
The ones that cover your grave...
The number of years you spent in pain...
They know the knight in you is still mightier
than the wave...

It took so much to see,
You've started living in me..
From time to time you come and go,
When the sun shines bright, when there's snow!!

Home of a Newly Broken Heart

As soon as you left, the curtains closed, the bed softened even more... the candles blew off, the sun tried to peep in while burning to its core... my room messed itself up, way more than before!! My make up bag exchanged glances to say- "No, you're not a whore!" My weighing machine couldn't help but laugh, my soft toys tried hard to offer me a new love... My books, they smirked their way to make space for a new friend, my perfume no longer waited for yours to blend!! My shower heated up the water a little stronger, my coziest clothes knew it was time once again for them to cover!! My mirror- my tears, my scars, my smile, my hopelessness it bore. My door- I begged but she decided to never open to you anymore!!

Outstanding

As for the moon, it stays right where it is supposed to be, right where it promises to be... a little too perfect and carefree! On the nights it isn't there, I know it's only the 'hide and seek' that keeps us up and makes the anxious wait only fair... Trying to hold on to the nuances that are not bright enough to light up an entire city, but bright enough to stand out in the darkness of half a galaxy.... In my eyes, I behold thee as the most beautiful and unshaken softly lit cotton far away from me

Hand-Made

My favorites in this whole wide world are few...
It's definitely not you,
You who felt every heart-beat of yours talking to
mine,
You who took every opportunity to make my
eyes shine,
You who took me to places I was too scared to
go to,
You who took me to happy places when my
hands were turning blue...
You were capable of so many things in such
short spans of time,
You knew very well you were more to me than
any diamond or dime,
You were my breeze and my coffee hue,
You painted a whole new picture of me, anew!!
You gave a new life and left...
Of the conventions that made us different, you
left my world bereft!!

BROKEN

Yes the moon was there,
Yes I found time with you to spare,
Yes the branches protected us,
Yes the hands slid into each other's,
Yes we sang together,
Yes we had a bad hangover,
Yes the summer breeze was slow,
Yes we were going with the flow,

But my beating heart was holding on to his
memories tight, my soul was hugging me with
all its might, my being slowly leaning into
yours, was being pulled back by his thoughts,
my thoughts filled up with his memories, my
breath felt him around me... I decided to part
with you, I decided to be with me, I decided on
my happiness with him over my happiness with
you, I decided to rather wait than to go to the
next stop, I decided to be in love with he who
held my hand when I was four!!

TWO CENTS

Today a drop, tomorrow an ocean,
You take a yard stick,
A measuring tape,
Fetching an estimate??
Those marks,
Those scratches and scars,
Those lines where the needle sewed the skin
together...
Those wrinkles and the hollows by the white
collar,
Them moles - you think you have it all figured
out?
The asset, the merit, the class...
Your constant check to see is she up there?
Did she have a fall?

The ups and falls in my universe will never be in
the same set as yours. My deepest scars are
hidden by the flawless parts of skin you kissed
last night. My dreams are not hidden by them
pink shades that you thought belonged to me.
Judging is inevitable but to judge someone you
say you are fond of is like a mother abandoning
her child!!

HYMNS

Show us the path to heal,
We have learnt a little more of how to feel!! A
humble prayer, a wish,
Restore humanity and peace
In pajamas and a naked heart,
Feelings and art,

The simplest of wish we make,
The chain of punishments can we break?

We have learnt the lesson,
You are all creation and destruction

Within me I see the quest exploding,
Anxiety and excitement boiling... Will they ever
get to you,
Will you answer my prayers, few?

The drops of ink stain,
The pages I write in vain... Broken yet hanging
on...
Catching up, blinkers on...

BOXED

Blessed are the ones who can flow through time,
reading books,
The ones who can make emotions out of words,
brew feelings out of pages and wander out of
hopeless texts,
The ones who can take a bigger step towards life
being within a room,
The ones who are blind but can feel the varied
hues,
The ones who are capable of lurking through
thoughts, flying without wings,
The ones who can make a normal day lively,
The ones who are keeping up with the
extraordinary in a room,
The ones who don't fail to dream each day,
The ones who don't shy away from a new risk, a
new move-
All within the four walls of a room,
Now their new world,
Their canvas of art!!

STAGNANT

All of us want to start again,
Why do we wait till we think it's time?
All of us want to us to be loved,
Why do we gulp down the tears inside and put
up a smile?
All of us want to be better...
Why do we even force down the idea of
competing with others?
All of us want to live free,
Why do we- under their values and beliefs,
shudder?
All of us want to set our own rules...
Why don't we set values that don't nose into
another?
All of us want to be respected,
Why don't we clap louder for each other?
All of us want to be looked upon with empathy...
Why don't we make way for people when we
have a little more comfort?
All of us want the world to be a better place...
Why don't we just contribute more,
put in more effort?

INSIDES

On the insides of me,
I am still you,
On the insides of me,
I am becoming a little more of you,
On the insides of me,
I am trying to get through,
On the insides of me,
I am trying to not miss you,
On the insides of me,
I am trying to not give up on you,
On the insides of me,
I am seeing your love stuck like glue,
On the insides of me,
I see myself dwelling in you,
On the insides of me,
I am waiting again to meet you!! On the insides
of me,
I am chopping off negativity, to make a soft
home for you!!
On the insides of me,
I am giving up pride, to make a tender room for
you!!

Unsure

We are talking a little each night,
Texts popping,
You were becoming a habit,
The more we read, the more we demanded each
other's sight... The sun knew it all, so did the
moon,
We were drawing the blinds off -
A little late than usual in the mornings,
Leaving bed almost at noon... I wish we had that
longer,
That feeling of not knowing,
That dearth of responsibility,
The need to go yonder... Now that I wait for you
at the second table,
By the window of your favorite caffe,
I am glad we chose this place,
To show you my happy places, forgive me, I'm
still not capable!!

Vacay

Remember the days...
All it took was one last ride,
To be happy and gay,

Through the last lane,
Through the crossroads,
We didn't let our love go in vain,

No one could I let, but you...
Take the lead and decide...
Where we could head to... You would never let
your presence,
Overshadow mine,
You're the one who taught patience... If I tell
you, would you believe?
I was always too scared,
Too scared to take the leap... Along you came...
Held you tight, and let it all go,
You didn't control or tame!! Oh, what a journey
it has been,
Eyes open, eyes close- in a blink,
About the journey, you made me keen...
Destination is vague and gray...
As long as we ride together,
Our life would make a story of one long vacay!!

Nest

There had been clouds,
There had been snow....
There had been rains,
The sun-kissed glow!! Inside the four blue walls,
She explored something, what one could call a
home,
No one to judge,
No one to scrutinize the occasional falls,

Then came along a little pause,
She packed her bags,
Left to jaunt,
Perhaps her favorite hues were changing from
turquoise to rose,

Months passed by,
To her it was as if, time was "too much on time"
Some days were breathtaking,
Some made her cry... Achievements came along,
So did punishments...
No breaks, her feet wouldn't stop,
They were singing their own song!! For no
rhyme or reason, one fine day,
She stopped to look up-
Look up at the blue sky,

It was as if something was calling out,
reminding her of the hue Celeste,

The u-turn was inevitable,
She was already missing doing nothing...
Just being who she was,
Not a soul to judge, to tell-tale... So she
returned,
Returned to the messed up bed, the huge
blankets,
The coffee stains,
The cushions that kept her anchored,

She never left,
This time, she was here to stay,
The broken blinds,
Forgave her for being imperfect... Her
ink-stained t-shirts,
Weren't waiting to be cleaned,
Weren't wanting to be paired-up,
With the best of her skirts!! Perhaps this wasn't
the best...
There could not have been any comparison with
the world outside,
There could definitely be no other placc to be,
other than the place that built her...
It was her abode, she was because it was- her
own nest!!

Sailors in the Fish Bowl

These small paper boats,
I have made out of the money we saved,
Shows what mattered to us both... The little
candles by the window,
I have lit out of the only match stick,
Shows how our bodies merged into one
shadow!! The little boxes of your favorite snack,
I have stocked up with our kitchen cupboard,
Shows how I was waiting for you to come
back!! These little pillows you have rested your
head on now...
I have changed the covers to beige...
Shows how your chest loves kissing my brow!!
These windows that have the same sight,
I have drawn the curtains to - smile,
Shows how we have been traveling through the
dark and the bright!! These calendars that have
the other plans,
I have scratched out and how!!
Shows I am sure of you, from now on, you
belong to my clan...

Discourse

You tell me I dream too much,
Were you believing we are happening? Now?
Existence has only been in your selfish
thoughts...
I am but a bubble of your thoughts- soon to
burst!! You tell me I believe in petty emotions...
Were you feeling me holding you?
It was a thread of hope only you were sewing...
I was not even validating it in our conversations!

You tell me I cry at every little inconvenience,
Toxic minds don't know how to prioritize...
Not even sorry to have been blessed with souls,
Whose normalcy to you means high
maintenance!!

PARCHED

Missing the times when I used to be,
Free from the hassle of pretentious shows,
Back when I was comfortable crying and
carefree,
It didn't matter how perfect the eyeliner strokes
were... There was you and there was this
feeling...
The ordinary chores sprinkled with magic,
There was a voice inside killing,
One by one the voices outside the walls -tragic...
Now that there's no you and me,
I smile a lot,
I laugh too, at things silly...
My world- a little less messy it has got!! The
small talk and the chittering,
Nights are as hard as days..
Some of them, I found myself shivering!!
My skin is covered with frays... Oh but those
were the times,
When you promised to come back,
My teardrops believed those lies,
They won't leave my eyes, you can hear... my
heart still cries!!

INTANGIBLE

Why is the line between letting go and
forcing oneself to let go so thin?

By the dungeon walls of the old city, holding
her phone she erased the text message she
wrote, she was aware of what his silence
would mean,

There is only so much the gift of luxury
could do,

Moments of despise were not few and in
them here travel tickets, brands and
perfectly painted nails would be friends too!!
Nonetheless his thoughts would hurl in and
gush down her cheeks from time to time,

Was he feeling it all too? Was he scared
she wasn't holding his hand through the
tumultuous and the fine?

It's true some souls meet to bring out the
epitome of best in each other,

Why is it through pain that the helm of
success, ripped apart they discover?

Can success and goals really measure-

The happiness and the satisfaction of a
soul's company and pleasure?

In this weary world where "letting go" is a
sport,

The intangible bond between you and
another soul, would you cherish? would you
court?

FRENZIED UTOPIA

Behind the broken pieces of the mirror glass,
you reflect me...
Beyond the frenzy of my messed hair, my
broken mood, you drive me to be crazy!!

Within the closed walls, you are with me but
another soul locked-up...
You would never miss a chance to catch my
vibes or swallow down desserts from my
favorite ice-cream tub!!

A little antique; a little bored of the same stories,
that I keep going back to,
You drive me insane, blow off candles, bake
new concoctions, take me places new...

It's magic how we do not need a single clock -
we have lost all sense of time...
We wake up when the world sleeps, playing by
the rules - to us is a crime,

If love was a mystery, we would be the most
inquisitive yet ignorant students,
The bars of companionship and faith we raise...
in our cage there is but no lament!!

The strings you pull, the buttons get torn...
A time or two we lay hopeless and mourn... -

Dread the times, we feel insecure and suffocate
on hope...
It feels like our past still stabs us, our throats get
choked...

Relentlessly, still we learn and grow,
We choose our friends, fate is left to pick the
foes...

Days and nights pass by in the blink of an eye,
To evolve with you, will there ever be enough
time??

REGENERATION

She started to feel the change, the change in her
decisions-
The change in the kind of music she listened to,
the change in the cravings of her taste buds;

She was pulling down the crocheted clothes that
covered the mirrors,
Flushing down the gazillion beauty pills and the
fake-promisingly products;

She was reading the book of fables, her mother
would read out to her, when she was a child;
She was coloring books, solving puzzles again-
she wanted to forget being old and wise!! She
was watching the moon change its shape and
color over the nights,
What felt lonely once, started feeling like
reaching new heights;

She was allowing the sun rays, into her room
every morning,
The windows were being opened again, the
curtains with the breeze flowing;

She was perpetually letting go of all the thoughts
depressing,
Slowly but steadily she was healing!

It was easier for her now than ever before,
When Mother Earth was resurrecting, she was
regenerating, she couldn't have asked for more!!

INEVITABLE

Sometimes it is inevitable,
Sometimes it is not about you,
Sometimes it is not about perseverance,
Sometimes it is about consistency, about being
stable!! Sometimes it can be about how cozy
your bed is,
Sometimes it can be about the aroma of baked
cookies,
Sometimes it can be about the comfort of the
flannel,
Sometimes, perhaps, it is about the softness of
the kiss!! Sometimes it is not about the chances
you lose because you're not privileged,
Sometimes it is not about the wrong decisions
you made,
Sometimes it is the other days that are still for
you to explore,
Sometimes it is destiny deciding the better or the
worse, the life you live!! Sometimes it is
stopping them from entering and leaving when
they want,
Sometimes it is about building walls customized
for your own insecurities,
Sometimes it is about barriers that define your
love for the child in you,

Sometimes it is about filtering out the best
version, not letting them daunt!! Sometimes it is
the small things that make you strong,
Sometimes it is the toil that you need to break
free from,
Sometimes it is about staring at wind chimes
when the breeze blows,
Sometimes it is about recalling, life will go on!!